Broken Butterflies

Broken Butterflies

By Sarah Wilt

Charleston, SC
www.PalmettoPublishing.com

Broken Butterflies
Copyright © 2021 by Sarah Wilt

First Edition

Hardcover ISBN: 978-1-63837-193-9
Paperback ISBN: 978-1-63837-194-6
eBook ISBN: 978-1-63837-195-3

Contents

Introduction

Hello to broken butterflies. Your shattered wings and glass
     shards stain the past to guide the weak.
You crawled up as a caterpillar, dangled a cocoon on a cliff; hot
     tar was underneath.

But you bloomed into a butterfly and flew away to see the sun;
you thought it fun to ride it to safety.
But when you got closer, your wings began to burn.
All you wanted was for it to not hurt.
Why does it hurt?
All you ever wanted was to fly away like a bird.

You just wanted to see your self-worth,
but the sun blinded you instead of guided you,
and you dove down underneath,
staring at the moon in a pile of roses that you laid.

The moon wouldn't hurt you, but you lost trust from the sun.
It beckoned and it called you, but you decided to run.
The moon cried its tears, and it gave its light away.
You couldn't see its intentions. Were they the same as the day?

You slept through the moon, but you awoke for the sun.

Droplets

Two water droplets parallel to each other,
Cascading down my windshield,
Eternities apart.
He is trying to touch her, but she is too far.

The path they follow, bumpy and jagged,
Deformed by the wind that runs them ragged.

Further down they slide.
Suddenly, they collide,
Merged into one.

Soul binding, they dance down the hill of glass.
Their cuts and bumps and bruises are now things of the past.

Oh, Won't You Be Mine?

You feel like trying a sweet treat for the first time—the flavor
    isn't something you're expecting but is still delicious,
unexpected, wonderful.
You feel like lying on the beach in the sun and closing your
    eyes while the sun hugs you with its rays,
warm, comforting, relaxing.
You feel like driving down an empty road, watching the sun
    rise while listening to your favorite song,
breathtaking, thrilling.
You feel like falling asleep to the sounds of the rain or a thun-
    derstorm,
nostalgic.
You feel like the first day of fall, when it gets cooler from the
    scorching, suffocating heat,
refreshing, relieving.
You feel like dancing in a meadow with nothing but you and
    the universe in company with the flowers.

You feel like freedom.
You feel like home.

Love Letters from the Sun and Moon

Sweet sun of mine, you are bright and bold and warm
and 150 million kilometers away.
I admire you from afar
as we switch places, night and day.
I hate to steal your spotlight,
but you love to make me shine.
When you stand behind me, I brighten up.
It reminds me you are mine.
Oh, sweet sun, you are so warm to me.
No matter how far away you are, you are my everything.

Moon of mine, you are cold, dark, and docile.
You control the waves of the sea,
and although you are not as bright as me,
I'm enchanted by your beauty.

You are captivating, gravitationally alluring.
You stun the ones who blissfully roam the earth at night.
You are a wondrous, otherworldly sight.
I will stand behind you to brighten you up for all to see,
to show the world what your beauty is to me.

Feathers

A lonesome white feather waltzed in the wind,
plucked from an angel's wing.

The last sweet words of sentiment danced off the
tongue of our beloved friend.
As the last breath they took landed on their cheeks to a
    smile.
"Weep not, sweet child.
I am happy and at peace in my bed of clouds."

The passing was quiet, but the grief rang loud.
The feather flew through the window and onto their heart,
and a million more feathers embraced the body in
deep slumber.

The feathers lifted up to depart,
then scattered across the room all over the floor.
The bed was now empty, a body to grieve no more,

and the cold fall wind whispered and hushed.
The silent sobs of sorrow bounced off the casket at ten
to the next hour

as the tender, sweet hands of loved ones by the casket
set down a bundle of feathers,
not flowers.

I Got What I Wanted

I got what I wanted.
Though it's just a memory,
I find it so lovely.
I feel less lonely
the moment I think of it.

I got what I wanted.
Although it's not pretty,
I find it so lovely.
It makes me so happy
the moment I look at it.

I got what I wanted.
Although it's not pricey,
I find it so lovely.
Just makes me feel at home
the moment I touch it.

I got what I wanted.
Although it's not flashy,
I find it so lovely.
It doesn't do anything,

just makes me so warm
the moment I cling to it.

I got what I wanted.
It's just a photo
of when I was younger
and so innocent.
It makes me feel safe.
And though I can't live it,
I can still see it
and cherish the serenity
the moment I want to be again.

Honey-Eyed Angel

The aromas of vanilla and honey gratify
the cloudy and soft voice resounding in my head.
You uphold me when I start to dwindle.
You are the light the guides me out of the dark cave of deso-
   lation.

I plea you never retire.
I'm aware you are persevering,
but you don't have to alone.

Oh, sweet honey-eyed angel, please don't fight alone.
Recall that I won't let you slip.
Commemorate our friendship and succumb to my arms.

I will carry you, even if I am not strong.

Confined

Confined in a cage
Writhing in unrest
Accosted by the fumes of my rage
Tipping over the crest

A mind falling ill, with the flick of a switch
Now irrecoverable
Train of thought now unhitched
Slow-moving feelings, now unreliable

False remedies giving false hope
Train of thought now lies stranded
Nerves frayed like the end of a rope
Therapy is uncandid

The thoughts that plague my mind
Will decay my soul with time

If There's a Light at the End,
It's in Your

His warm and alluring grin makes the cold and desolate
    depths of my mind
illuminate with joy.
Gripped by the serene laughter, I plummet into a consoling
    crib of blossoms.
His arms are ornamental on me, like a pond filled with koi.
I'm in love, and that's not the problem.
I'm apprehensive when he decides to take his leave,
akin to those before him.
When he has gone, am I prepared to grieve?

Shattered Eyes

In the mirror all I see
the last thing I want to be

Reflection, reflection
Broken glass
Reflecting, reflecting
shattered past

Asphyxiated by my antipathy
Self-despise is my own demise
Don't need your sympathy
I'm tranquil, submerging in my cries

Why do they try to break something already broken?
Their apologies stay unspoken

Unwavering self-reproach
Wallow not in anguish
Tending to souls will be my approach
Selflessness will be my love language

Under the Willow

Sundrops kiss the forest leaves
Honeydew and buzzing bees
Ponds of golden koi and dreams
Well-wished coins and sky-bussed trees

All fun and games
All stays the same

Book of blank pages
Stories in the making
Welcome to a happy place
Where nothing ever ages

Silk grass blades
Bubbling riverbanks
Cooling willow shade
Streams from which the elk drank

Under the willow
Is where I'll stay
Under the willow
Where everything is okay

Burning Coloring Books

I lit them all aflame
covered up my tracks
so I wouldn't have to face my shame
I guess that now my gig is up, close the curtain on the act

I burned my coloring books
I'll admit, I cried
I burned them all away
so I could save my pride

I tore up my stuffed animals and threw them in the trash
I locked away my pacifiers and broke my sippy cups in half

And it's so sad
and it makes me mad
that I had to burn my coloring books
I had to say goodbye
I burned my coloring books because my secret I couldn't hide

Drowned White Rose

the torn-up white rose in the meadow
around the field of flowers
you turned the corner and befriended me
too scared to ruin their petals
but the flower I was, you wanted to hold me
out of the flowers you chose
the one you chose was falling apart
the petals were falling off
and bleeding red out of the heart
you held me in your palm and watered me with your love
"beware of the thunderstorm" cried the ill-minded dove
but my ears did not listen
because when I looked into your eyes
they just…glistened
but the more you watered me to make me grow
I wilted more
I was flooded with this water
a weed you began to sow
the seed was packed with anger, miscommunication, and
    blame
I'm the victim
but the culprit of the crime

it got harder to breathe, the more you drowned me with time
and like the torn-up fool I was, I stayed and let it slide
but I'm screaming as you rip my roots up and don't even
    realize
I'm too afraid to cry out that you are drowning me when you
    think you're watering me
but how can I say anything?

I am only a white withered rose with a mouth full of water

Dark and Light

dark light
the sun kisses the back side of the moon to create a spotlight,
    even when the sun is not present there's beauty in the
    darkness

invisible plain sight
the moon is alone and unseen and not shown
but the sun is showered with love and admiration, yet the sun
    still sees her when no one else will
he will show her to everyone who sees him

moon and sun
yin and yang
no matter where you go, opposites find a way to coincide
and eventually create beauty

Does It Hurt?

Does it hurt?
Does it hurt to let them rise above the surface?
You try to choke them down, but it's not worth it.

Does it get cold,
being locked away in your mind, in a cage,
no way out of the dark, all alone all afraid?
You're left to rot there as you age.

Does it make you tired,
wanting to let go,
waiting for the air to feel thin again?
It's so thick, you can't breathe,
and every time you want to cry,
your heart hurts and you grieve.
You grieve for yourself
because no one else will.
No one else will feel what you feel,
and that's real.
They give you powdered pellets to take away the pain,
but more pain is all you gain when you start to rely,
rely instead of try.

The dust at the bottom of the bottle is not a wake-up call.
It's a reminder to go get more
so you can feel warm and numb.
And they say it's dumb,
but they save you.

But you're running out of time before they kill you.
Is it worth the risk?
To wake up and feel like this?
You'd rather go to sleep and feel nothing at all.
So why are we afraid of dying?

Are you exhausted from crying?
Another empty bottle.
Your mind is scrambled,
your life you gambled away
to feel this way.

And you wouldn't even care if it took you out.
That's all you ever think about.
When the day comes, you pop it in your mouth, and you're
    done.
There is no more cage
because what's the point of a cage without a bird to sing in
    it?
You stopped singing.
You stopped dreaming.

You won't even bother to open your eyes.
You gave up; you can't even cry.

Why didn't you try?
You got back up when they yelled, saying you weren't good
    enough.
You got back up time and time again,
but no one would help you win.
The pills are your only friend.
Take them before the voices start again.
Take them before you start shaking and breaking.
Don't you dare break down.
You don't want to look weak,
but you are.
They control you.
They define you.
They revive you.
They will end you.
As much as they made you,
why'd you let them take you?

The Clouds

The clouds were striving to write your name,
but the sun pierced through them and tore their aim.

I looked to the grass to see my feet,
to find the ash of the bridge you burned under me.

My head refuses to turn west
because great things are set ahead for the best.

The intricacy of the silence is beautiful.
I'm neighbored by the love that is truthful.

The clouds abdicated, failed their attempt,
and the sun is still beaming.
Now I'm focused on me. I'm kempt,
ceased nightmares, inbound dreaming.

I won't miss what we had.
I won't be sad.

The Moon and Never Back

I fell
Fell so hard for the rose-colored glass
I fell
Fell so fast for the lies
Now the I-love-yous are in our past
I can love me, and it's true
I'll know that for a fact
unlike the way it was with you

I love you
To the moon and never back

I'll leave you with all the love that we had
I won't look your way
Not a thought of what we were
Because you thought it wouldn't hurt
To lie and deceive and make me believe that it was meant to
    be
Well, I won't cry
And you know why?
Because I'm at peace
With loving me

I love you
To the moon and never back

I'm not sad, throwing away what we had
I cared for you, but you didn't care for me
I was holding you when you cried
But you couldn't hold it forever
All the lies you tried to hide

Now I know that you weren't for me
Now I know it was never meant to be

But I'm okay
I'm living my life
Somebody else will come along and make me their wife
Somebody will eventually treat me right

I wish you well
I hope you find peace and crawl your way up from hell
I hope you find
Someone worth your time
Because after all those months, you wasted mine

I love you
To the moon and never back

I'm not sad, throwing away what we had
I cared for you
But you didn't care for me
But I'm alright with that
I'm loving me, and that's my peace

CPSIA information can be obtained
at www.ICGtesting.com
Printed in the USA
BVHW061522020222
627784BV00020B/1898

9 781638 371946